What Camping Can Teach Us

Life's Lessons Learned from the Great Outdoors

WILLOW CREEK PRESS

Published by Willow Creek Press
P.O. Box 147
Minocqua, Wisconsin 54548

Photo Credits;
p2 © Mark Newman/AlaskaStock.com
p3 © Ron Sanford/Corbis
p4 © Joe McDonald/Corbis
p7 © Margo Taussig Pinkerton/AlaskaStock.com
p8 © Patrick Frischknecht/Peter Arnold, Inc.
p12 © Gary W. Carter/Corbis
p13 © Richard Hamilton Smith/Corbis
p14 © James Baigrie/GettyImages
p17 © Tom Bol/AlaskaStock.com
p19 © Lisa & Mike Husar/www.teamhusar.com
p20 © John R. Ford
p22 © Christof Wermter/zefa/Corbis
p23 © W. Perry Conway/Corbis
p24 © Michael DeYoung/AlaskaStock.com
p26 © Kenny Bahr/The Image Finders
p27 © Michael DeYoung/AlaskaStock.com
p29 © Barbara Peacock/Corbis
p32 © David Job/AlaskaStock.com

Design: Donnie Rubo
Printed in the USA

"Camping: the art of getting closer to nature while getting away from the nearest cold beverage, hot shower and flush toilet."

-Author unknown

"Shelter comes in
all shapes, sizes
and forms...

...but a tent is best for camping."

-Jillanne Consie

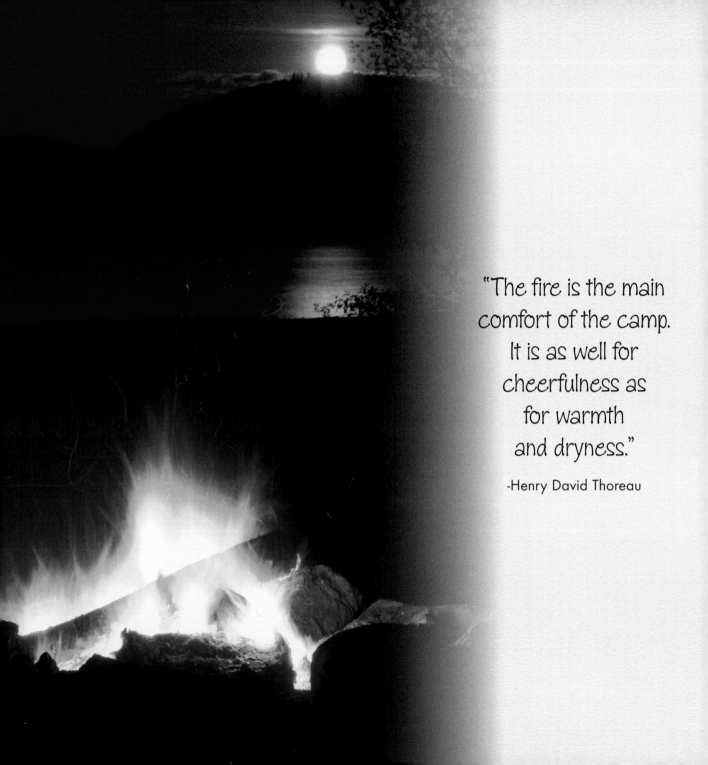

"The fire is the main comfort of the camp. It is as well for cheerfulness as for warmth and dryness."

-Henry David Thoreau

"Families are like fudge...
mostly sweet with a few nuts."

-Author unknown

"I don't have to look up my family tree,
because I know that I'm the sap."

-Fred Allen

"By plucking
the petals, you
do not gather the
beauty of the flower."

-Tagore

"Nature is like an enormous restaurant."

-Woody Allen

"Everything
and anything...

...tastes better outdoors."

-Author unknown

"Hunger is the best sauce in the world."

-Francis Beaumont

"Everyone
must believe
in something...

...I believe I'll go canoeing."

-Henry David Thoreau

"If you think you're too small to be effective,
you've never been in bed with a mosquito."

-Betty Reese

"Whoa, something smells stinky! Oh, wait, it's me."

-Barney Gumble, The Simpsons

"The biggest fish ever caught are those that get away."

-Eugene Field

"If people concentrated on the really important things in life, there'd be a shortage of fishing poles."

-Doug Larson

"Call it a clan, call it a network, call it a tribe, call it a family. Whatever you call it, whoever you are, you need one."

-Jane Howard

"Those who do not read are no better off than those who cannot."

-Proverb

"It always rains on tents. Rainstorms will travel thousands of miles against prevailing winds to rain on a tent."

-Dave Berry

"There is only one pretty child in the world,
and every mother has it."

-Chinese Proverb

"Anyone who keeps the ability to see beauty never grows old."

-Franz Kafka

"Let the tent
be struck."

-Robert E. Lee

"We people in camp are merely big children,
wayward and changeable."

-Rutherford Birchard Hayes

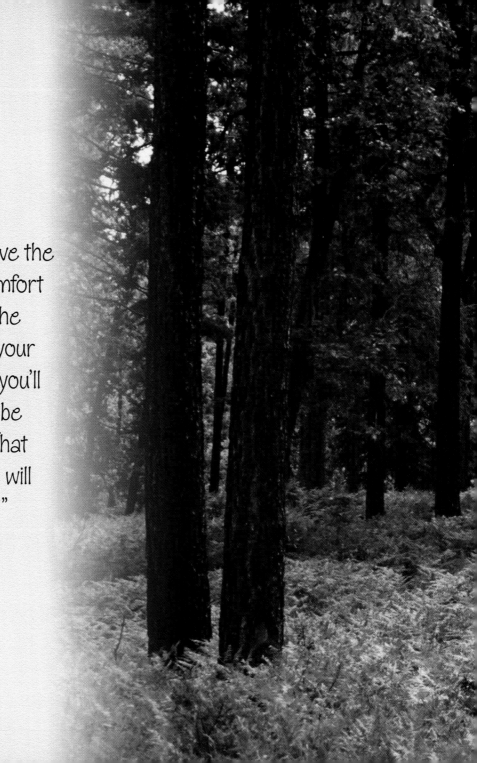

"You have to leave the city of your comfort and go into the wilderness of your intuition. What you'll discover will be wonderful. What you'll discover will be yourself."

-Alan Alda